I Love it Here
South-East Asia

Text and photography by Tony Watts

Consultant: Sandy Walsh
Designer: Pauline Yong of Asher Concepts Pte. Ltd.
Thanks to: Jacqueline Fury and Audrey Simon

First published in 2007 by Luxe Life Pte Ltd
220 Tagore Lane #03-01
Singapore 787600

Correspondence to:
PO Box 189
Tanglin Post Office
Singapore 912407
contact@loveitthere.com
www.loveitthere.com

Paperstock used in the production of this book is from wood grown in sustainable forests and maufactured using a non-acid
bleaching process. Ink is soy based in an alcohol-free printing solution.

Luxe Life Pte. Ltd. supports Yejj, which provides training and employment for disadvantaged young people in Cambodia.
Log onto www.yejj.com for more information

ISBN 981-05-6306-X

Printed in Singapore by KHL Pte. Ltd.

>>introduction

In many ways this book was born out of frustration.

Honest information about hotels and resorts in South-East Asia is almost non-existent. Vacations in the region are a lottery — sometimes you can luck into an undiscovered gem of a place, but for every hotel that excels there are dozens that fail to impress.

In the course of researching this book we have stayed in hundreds of hotels, and as a result are very demanding customers. The hotels featured here are the ones we recommend to friends, in the sincere belief that the surroundings, service, and style will win them over.

Each hotel featured is unique and extraordinary in some way, and none have paid to be included. They are not all created equal — some of the countries covered are relative newcomers to the luxury tourism market and in these cases we have mentioned the properties that impressed the most. The good news is that the industry is improving constantly.

Now the only frustration is that we can't get back to them often enough.

About the rankings:

Every hotel included is here on merit, but some are better than others.

lifetime love — This is the real thing; true love. These hotels are the best you will find, and will keep you coming back.

lost weekend — The tumultuous affair. It makes your heart flutter to think about, but it couldn't last forever. These places are not perfect, but pretty close.

one-night stand — You know you shouldn't have but it was good, wasn't it? These are the places you might even revisit.

In any case, what's important is that you love it here.

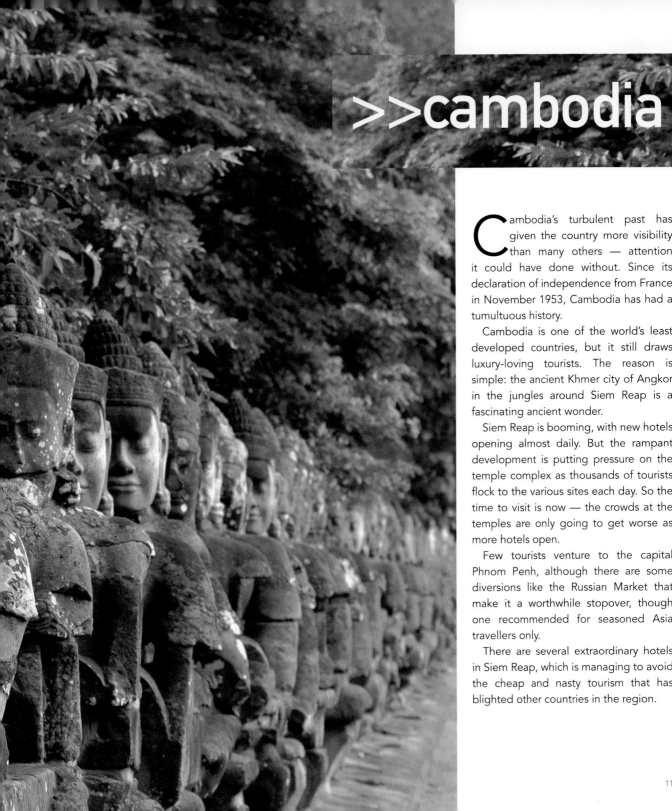

>>cambodia

Cambodia's turbulent past has given the country more visibility than many others — attention it could have done without. Since its declaration of independence from France in November 1953, Cambodia has had a tumultuous history.

Cambodia is one of the world's least developed countries, but it still draws luxury-loving tourists. The reason is simple: the ancient Khmer city of Angkor in the jungles around Siem Reap is a fascinating ancient wonder.

Siem Reap is booming, with new hotels opening almost daily. But the rampant development is putting pressure on the temple complex as thousands of tourists flock to the various sites each day. So the time to visit is now — the crowds at the temples are only going to get worse as more hotels open.

Few tourists venture to the capital Phnom Penh, although there are some diversions like the Russian Market that make it a worthwhile stopover, though one recommended for seasoned Asia travellers only.

There are several extraordinary hotels in Siem Reap, which is managing to avoid the cheap and nasty tourism that has blighted other countries in the region.

Amansara

We have always had a slight aversion to the luxurious Aman chain. The hotels are spectacular and the service sets the standards, but the pricing can shock. At Amansara, a night's accommodation costs more than twice Cambodia's annual per capita income. Can it possibly be worth it?

The answer is an emphatic yes.

Because Angkor is so popular, lesser hotels in Siem Reap command high room rates too. But the Aman experience trounces the competition decisively.

Amansara organises personalised itineraries for its guests to tour the temple complex, taking in the sights they want to see and attempting to avoid the busloads of sightseers. This can mean early starts, but coffee and croissants delivered to the slick rooms after the wake-up call does take the sting out of them somewhat. And then you have the astounding temples almost to yourself in the relatively cool early morning hours.

After visiting the temples, you are free to relax at the peaceful grounds of the Amansara compound, which contrast starkly with the noise of the main road just outside. The staff seem almost telepathic in anticipating your needs, making the experience sublime.

Our room seemed to have been made up four times a day, yet we never saw any Aman staff entering or leaving, except to deliver that pre-dawn coffee.

If you want to see the ancient temples at Angkor, there is no better way to do it than by staying at Amansara. The premium for such a once-in-a-lifetime experience is well worth paying.

Amansara
address   Road to Angkor, Siem Reap
phone   +855 63 760-333
web   www.amanresorts.com
capacity 24 rooms
rates   US$650-875++

ranking - lifetime love
Small. Stunning. Perfect.

luxe
• Sublime service • The best way to see
the temples at Angkor

less luxe
• Pricing

best for
The address in Siem Reap. Tour the
temples, then relax around the pool.

✱ insider tip
Save up and stay here.

Raffles Hotel Le Royal

The Raffles property in Phnom Penh has too many rooms to feature here, although all is not lost.

The Art Deco façade may be heavy and imposing — rather like the government buildings across the street — but it hides the best part of the hotel.

The main building has the genuine 1920s period rooms; the north and south courtyards and garden wings are later additions.

These new wings mimic the look and style of the main building and enclose the pools in a large and private courtyard. But the rooms in the new wings are a bit disappointing in comparison with those in the main building, which offer some period atmosphere.

The upside of a large hotel like this is a good selection of places to eat and drink, notably the Restaurant Le Royal. The Elephant bar does a decent job of recreating a colonial-era feel, right down to the fact that you may end up next to someone obnoxious smoking a cigar.

A room in the main building is an experience, however, and arguably the best available in Phnom Penh.

Raffles Hotel Le Royal
address 92 Rukhak Vithei Daun Penh
         (off Monivong Boulevard)
         Sangkat Wat Phnom,
         Phnom Penh, Cambodia
phone   +855 23 981-888
web   www.raffles.com
capacity 170 rooms
rates   US$260-2,000+

Raffles Hotel Le Royal

ranking - lost weekend
There is a warmer welcome than the imposing façade suggests.

luxe
• Sense of history • Dining

less luxe
• The newer rooms are not so special

best for
The best address in Phnom Penh.

✳ insider tip
Rooms in the main wing are the pick.

21

FCC Angkor Hotel

The hotel room rates in Siem Reap are so high that you may think the hotel receptionist has misheard you — you only want a room for a night, not to buy the hotel.

That makes the FCC Angkor a find.

Most rooms in the two-storey hotel are clustered around the small pool. FCC Angkor offers smart, modern accommodation at a price that will not make you faint. The suites cost more but are more spacious than the standard rooms, which can feel a bit claustrophobic, and those nearest the pool feel less private.

FCC Angkor is an addition to the old French Ambassador's mansion, which is now the FCC Angkor Kitchen — the hottest restaurant in town. Very smart.

The FCC Angkor is not the last word in luxury, but the prices are reasonable in a town where they seem out of control. Its location is excellent and the ambience quite pleasant too.

FCC Angkor Hotel, Restaurant & Spa

address   Pokambor Avenue (next to the Royal Residence), Siem Reap
phone   + 855 63 760-280
web   www.fcccambodia.com
capacity   31 rooms
rates   US$99-330+ (Seasonal)

FCC Angkor Hotel

ranking - one-night stand
Small, funky and wallet-friendly.

luxe
• Relaxed surrounds
• Excellent restaurant

less luxe
• Small standard rooms

best for
The best way to see the Angkor temples if you are trying to stick to a budget.

✱ insider tip
Avoid claustrophobia — choose a suite.

Stay

Featured Hotels:
- Amansara
- FCC Angkor Hotel, Restaurant & Spa
- Raffles Hotel le Royal

Also:

HÔTEL DE LA PAIX
+ 855 63 966-000
Sivutha Boulevard
Siem Reap, Cambodia
www.hoteldelapaixangkor.com

One of the newest additions to the accommodation scene in Siem Reap, and almost certainly the funkiest, Hôtel de la Paix is attracting a fair amount of attention.

RAFFLES GRAND HOTEL D'ANGKOR
+855 63 963-888
1 Vithei Charles de Gaulle
Khum Svay Dang Kum
Siem Reap, Cambodia
www.raffles.com

Another grande dame Raffles hotel, the Grand Hotel d'Angkor is a landmark in Siem Reap and well worth visiting. Choose a room in the old wing for more atmosphere.

Eat

CAFÉ YEJJ
+855 12 543-360
170, Street 450
12310 Phnom Penh, Cambodia

This casual café right near the Russian market offers a respite from all that bargaining. A good place for lunch — sandwiches, salads and other café-style food — while doing the right thing by supporting disadvantaged youths.

FCC ANGKOR KITCHEN
+ 855 63 760-280
Pokambor Avenue,
Siem Reap, Cambodia

Occupying the entire second level of a restored colonial building, the modern interior of the FCC Angkor Kitchen is a stark contrast with the exterior, but it works very well. Dishes range from Cambodian to pizza and pasta, and come at reasonable prices.

KMER KITCHEN
+855 63 964-154
Alley behind Pub Street
Siem Reap, Cambodia

The address probably gives it away: Kmer Kitchen is hardly an upmarket joint, but the selection of local specialities and absurdly cheap prices make it a must if you're in Siem Reap. Your hotel's concierge will know it for sure.

MALIS RESTAURANT
+855 23 221-022
136, Norodom
12301 Phnom Penh, Cambodia

Choose to sit in the garden courtyard of this contemporary Khmer reastaurant for the best ambience — the garden bar is also a good place for a drink. You can't go wrong with the food here: it's all good, though the wine selection is limited.

RESTAURANT LE ROYAL
+855 23 981-888
Raffles Hotel Le Royal
92 Rukhak Vithei Daun Penh (off Monivong)
Boulevard Sangkat Wat Phnom,
Phnom Penh, Cambodia

Arguably Phnom Penh's best restaurant, Restaurant Le Royal is certainly one of it's most formal. The menu offers French and Royal Cambodian cuisine, and the service is faultless, though you pay for it.

See

The temples at Angkor are the only reason most tourists visit Cambodia. They are utterly stunning, but can be crowded too, particularly Angkor Wat. The so-called lesser temples are no less impressive, and if you time your visit right you may have one nearly to yourself.

Our favourites include the Bayon, the gates of Angkor Thom and Ta Prohm, which is overgrown with trees. The sheer scale of Angkor Wat cannot fail to impress, despite the thousands of tourists visiting daily.

>>indonesia

If you believe the news headlines, Indonesia is torn by strife and best avoided. Don't be put off: at the right places in Indonesia you will be treated to absolute luxury and enjoy the sort of peace and tranquillity you only dream about.

Indonesia comprises more than 17,000 islands but only one of them — Bali — gets much of the tourism attention. It has unjustly earned a reputation as a destination for drunkard Australian teenagers and surfies, though the tragic bombings have scared most western tourists away.

But if you avoid trashy Kuta Beach, the rest of Bali is sensational. Seminyak, on the southern coast, and Ubud, in the hills, are the upmarket centres and the best choices for a deluxe holiday.

One trip to Bali will have you believing that hospitality was invented there.

But that is not to suggest you will not get a warm welcome elsewhere in Indonesia, and there is plenty to see and do. So long as you pay attention to travel advisories and exercise a little common sense, Indonesia will captivate you.

The Balé

Unexpected is about the only way to describe The Balé on the southern tip of Bali at Nusa Dua.

What makes The Balé different is the sparse style of architecture. Unadorned lines are not what you expect of villas in Bali, but that is what you get with the sandstone-walled pavilions at The Balé. Under their traditional *alang alang* grass roofs, the rooms are simple, comfortable and very well designed.

Strangely, the *balé* in each pavilion has a roof that looks like a concrete wedding cake rather than an *alang alang* feature, but the massive daybed, deckchairs and mini bar help compensate for that.

A small patch of emerald-green grass shaded by a fragrant frangipani tree leads to each villas' private pool, which is accessible directly from the bathroom too. Our villa overlooked the Face restaurant, which meant less privacy and noise from the kitchen — a shame in an otherwise peaceful location.

The beach is a short walk down the relatively quiet public road on which The Balé sits. It is a favourite among knowledgeable surfers for its offshore reef break. The sand here is about the best we've seen in Bali, and a temple perched on the cliff at the end of the beach adds a suitably exotic Balinese touch.

The main attraction of The Balé is its modern take on a traditional Balinese pavilion. You will want to lock yourself away in your villa for a few days.

The Balé

address	P.O. Box 76, Jalan Raya Nusa Dua Selatan, Nusa Dua 80363, Bali, Indonesia
phone	+62 361 775-111
web	www.thebale.com
capacity	20 rooms
rates	US$480-800++

The Balé

ranking - lifetime love
How much style can you bear?

luxe
• Arguably the most contemporary rooms in Bali • Chic, simple landscaping • Close to one of the island's prettiest and quietest beaches • Personal butler service

less luxe
• Expensive dining • Some pavilions could have more privacy • Little apart from the beach nearby

best for
Sitting quietly on the giant daybed in your own balé, only emerging to dip in your private pool. Bliss.

✳ insider tip
Ask for a room away from the noisy kitchen.

Ibah

Position, position, position is how a real estate agent would sell the Ibah site. It makes an ideal base from which to explore Ubud, the cultural and artistic centre of Bali.

The Ibah villas line one side of the Tjampuhan River valley at the edge of Ubud. The centre of town is a short walk away, but an Ibah driver will drop you there anytime you want. Fortunately, the valley setting is far enough from the main road that the traffic noise is inaudible, and the villas close to the river are treated to the sound of running water too.

With only 15 rooms, Ibah is small enough for extremely personal service. When you see the room service prices, you might be tempted not to leave your private compound at all.

The rooms vary fairly wildly in style and quality, however. Our favourites are those with private gardens, including the lower level duplex rooms and the stand-alone suites. Unfortunately, the lower level rooms don't have the traditional vaulted *al'ang al'ang* thatched ceilings.

Each time we stay at Ibah, we spend plenty of time imagining how the rooms could be redecorated. Nevertheless, the magic of the peaceful location, the uncrowded pool, and the artfully mossy walls and stone carvings scattered through the pretty grounds keep us coming back.

Not perfect, but pretty close.

Ibah Luxury Villas & Spa

address	Campuhan, Ubud, Bali, Indonesia
phone	+62 361 974-466
web	www.ibahbali.com
capacity	15 rooms
rates	US$215-500++

ranking - lifetime love
Peaceful and magical. Traditionally styled villas close to the arts centre of Bali.

luxe
• Walking distance to the centre of town, if you don't want to use the complimentary, on-call shuttle • Brilliant and inexpensive breakfasts • Truly friendly service • Close to some fantastic restaurants

less luxe
• Long flights of stairs to some rooms • Décor is tired in places • Limited closet space

best for
Explore the town of Ubud, then retreat to a private, quiet Ibah villa.

✱ insider tip
The rooms with private gardens are the best (the Ibah Suite and single room Pool Villa are our favourites).

The Legian

Individual villas are the norm for upscale properties on Bali, which makes The Legian somewhat unusual. The four-storey concrete structure has Balinese touches to its design, without being overwhelming.

The Legian is more of a smart city hotel transplanted to a beachfront setting, which is a good thing given that the beach at Seminyak is not the most beautiful in Asia. The Legian is well situated at the geographic centre of the best restaurants and bars on the island however.

The large rooms feature slick bathrooms and so many lighting options it gets confusing, and all have decent-sized balconies facing the ocean. The Legian's Studio rooms lack storage space, but are much larger than the name suggests.

The pool is spectacular — cascading over two levels towards the ocean — although it feels a bit small for such a large hotel. It is illuminated by flame in the evening, which makes dinner in the restaurant quite a special event.

The Legian has responded to the demand for villas in Bali, with 11 available across the road at The Club At The Legian. Each walled villa has its own pool as well as a *balé* for outdoor lounging and dining. A restaurant and a 35-metre lap pool solely for Club guests add to the atmosphere of exclusivity.

There is a scene of sorts in Seminyak, and The Legian is ideally positioned to enjoy it. Its comfort, style and superior service make it the best choice in the area.

The Legian & The Club at The Legian

address	Jalan Laksmana, Seminyak Beach 80361, Bali, Indonesia
phone	+62 361 730-622
web	www.ghmhotels.com
capacity	67 rooms; 11 villas; one beach house
rates	US$380-2,500++ (Seasonal)

ranking - lost weekend
A chic hotel in a beachfront setting.

luxe
• Spacious and well-maintained rooms
• Exemplary service • Location could not be better for Balinese beachfront hotels

less luxe
• The food is pricey and breakfast could be better • Only has queen-size beds, even in the Club villas

best for
A perfect base from which to enjoy the local bar and restaurant scene by night and lazing on the beach by day.

* insider tip
The upper floors offer more privacy and have better ocean views.

Pulau Pangkil Kecil

ranking - lost weekend
An island all your own — could it get much better?

luxe
• Gorgeous natural scenery • Great food
• No need to put up with other people

less luxe
• No air-conditioning • Rustic villas will not suit everyone • The ferry trip is not a deluxe experience

best for
A holiday with a difference for a group of friends.

✱ insider tip
Book a masseuse for the day and really relax.

Pulau Pangkil Kecil
web   www.pangkil.com
capacity   Nine villas
rates   S$2,000-3,500 per night for one to10 people (Seasonal)

If you have ever dreamed of your own tropical island Pulau Pangkil Kecil can make that dream come true.

This is no regular resort; it's a whole island — and it is wholly yours to enjoy.

While the rustic Driftwood Palaces could hardly be described as the last word in luxury, they are functional and stylish, and the outdoor bathrooms offer what are possibly the best views from any bathroom in the world through the glassless window openings.

The island lies off the south-east coast of Bintan, so getting there is easy enough on the many ferries from Singapore.

The rates include meals, which the ever-helpful staff will serve whenever and wherever on the island you want.

Activities include fishing trips, picnics to neighbouring islands, as well as sailing dinghies and surf skis. There is a colourful reef, which is ideal for snorkelling too.

The villas are not available individually — you have to book the whole island — so Pangkil is essentially a destination for a group. But what a destination.

A truly unique experience and great value too.

Alila Ubud

The stunning pool at the Alila Ubud looks like a block of granite perched on the edge of the Ayung River gorge. It was the sight of this pool that first attracted us to the Alila Ubud — and it still takes our breath away.

Design does take a front seat here though. There is simply not enough poolside seating to accommodate all the Alila guests. Nevertheless, it is a pretty place to sit and admire the scenery while enjoying the scent of the fresh tuberoses at the end of the pool.

The Alila has 56 rooms in the main two-storey blocks. The Superior rooms are on the upper level and offer pitched ceilings and private balconies that overlook the river valley. The Deluxe rooms on the ground level have indoor/outdoor bathrooms and garden terraces. Unfortunately, the garden terraces are not entirely private and you will want to close the curtains unless you are an exhibitionist.

There are eight stand-alone villas (like the one pictured), and the best of these overlook the river valley. If you want complete privacy, choose one of these.

The name is a little misleading though — the Alila Ubud is set among rice terraces about half an hour's drive from the centre of Ubud town, which does make it fairly isolated. But it takes advantage of its location, with walking tours to the nearest village offering a glimpse of local colour.

Alila Ubud

address	Desa Melinggih Kelod, Payangan, Giyanyar, Bali 80572, Indonesia
phone	+62 361 975-963
web	www.alilahotels.com
capacity	56 rooms; eight villas
rates	US$240-450++

ranking - lost weekend

Breathe in the fresh air and enjoy splendid isolation.

luxe

• Stunning pool and great walking tours
• Listen to the temple activities across the gorge

less luxe

• The 30-minute drive to Ubud town can make you feel trapped • Standard rooms can feel cramped after an extended stay

best for

Isolation among the pretty rice terraces.

✱ insider tip

The Ayung River Villas offer the best views.

Banyan Tree Bintan

ranking - lost weekend
Absolute peace in stylish individual villas.

luxe
• Privacy of the villas • Uninterrupted ocean views • Friendly staff

less luxe
• Food is average and expensive
• Rack rates are stiff • Maintenance could be better

best for
Escaping from the rest of the world for a romantic weekend.

✱ insider tip
Choose the Seaview Jacuzzi villas for the best view and value.

Banyan Tree Bintan
address Site A4, Lagoi, Tanjong Said, Bintan Island, Indonesia
phone +62 770 693-100
web www.banyantree.com
capacity 70 rooms
rates US$470-1,450++

Bintan is the largest island in the Riau Archipelago, which is close to Singapore. Most visitors get to Bintan by fast ferry from Singapore, heading for Bintan Resorts on the northern coast of the island. The area has been almost totally cleared of Indonesian residents and is not a good choice if you want to experience some local culture.

The Banyan Tree Bintan has been well designed with this lack of local colour in mind: the individual villas are perfect for spending some time locked away from the rest of the world. The villas are situated on a rocky promontory and seem to have been designed to preserve most of the mature trees on the site.

The many different villa styles can make for a difficult choice. The Pool Villas are a bit of a waste for one couple, as they were designed for two couples to share. The Jacuzzi Villas are some of the smartest rooms we have come across, although their maintenance could be better.

If you must leave the comfort of the room, there are two pools that are never crowded, and a pleasant, if not spectacular beach to walk along, although in recent times it has seen the addition of another giant resort.

The beauty of the Banyan Tree Bintan is its combination of a lovely forest setting, the views out over the ocean and the solitude of the rooms.

Stay

Featured Hotels:
- Alila Ubud
- The Balé
- Banyan Tree Bintan
- Ibah Luxury Villas & Spa
- The Legian & The Club at The Legian
- Pulau Pangkil Kecil

Also:

AMANJIWO
+62 293 788-333
Borobudur, Magelang
Central Java, Indonesia
www.amanresorts.com
There is no better place to stay than Amanjiwo for exploring the ancient Buddhist temple at Borobudur, which is visible in the distance. Prices to match.

THE DHARMAWANGSA
+62 21 725-8181
Jalan Brawijaya Raya No. 26, Kebayoran Baru, Jakarta 12160, Indonesia
www.the-dharmawangsa.com
If you must go to Jakarta, you may as well do it in style — and that means the Dharmwangsa.

DOWNTOWN VILLAS
+62 361 736-464
Jalan Pura Dalem 9d, Seminyak,
Bali 80361, Indonesia
www.downtownbali.com
Nine modern villas with pools and kitchens (and room service if you want it) right in the heart of the Seminyak shopping district.

FOUR SEASONS PRIVATE ESTATE
+62 361 701-010
Jimbaran, Denpasar,
Bali 80361, Indonesia
www.fourseasons.com
Vast, separate villas inside walled compounds for supreme privacy, with Four Seasons service. Priced accordingly.

HYATT REGENCY YOGYAKARTA
+62 274 869-123
Jalan Palagan Tentara Pelajar
Yogyakarta 55581, Indonesia
www.hyatt.com
Spell it however you please — Jogyakarta is at the epicentre of Java's tourism business and the Hyatt is well placed to experience it all.

UMA UBUD
+62 361 972-448
Jalan Raya Sanggingan
Banjar Lungsiakan, Kedewatan
Ubud, Gianyar 80571, Bali, Indonesia
www.como.bz
Really slick, minimalist villas in Bali's cultural heartland. The focus is on holistic living with yoga retreats, reflexology, meditation and more.

Eat

KU DÉ TA
+62 361 736-969
Jalan Laksmana 9, Seminyak,
Bali, Indonesia
The place to be seen in Seminyak, offering

substance and style. The food and service are faultless and the beachfront location is brilliant, but the prices are truly First World.

MOSAIC
+62 361 975-768
Jalan Sanggingan, Ubud, Bali, Indonesia
The food is a well-executed fusion of French and modern American. The service is excellent and the garden setting is gorgeous.

See

UBUD TRAIL
Just about anywhere on Bali you will find something wonderful. We like to walk through the rice terraces around Ubud. A long trail starts at the temple at the Tjampuhan River and meanders through swaying grass, small villages and emerald-green rice terraces. Not recommended for people with limited mobility or who are squeamish about snakes.

BOROBUDUR
The Buddhist monument at Borobudur is impressive. This is the biggest tourist attraction in Java, so start early or risk being jostled in the crowds.

>>laos

Tiny, landlocked Laos has only appeared on tourist itineraries in the recent past, and arrivals of around a million a year means it lags well behind its higher-profile neighbours as a tourist destination.

If you think this means you will not see any other tourists on your travels, you'd be wrong. The UNESCO World Heritage listed city of Luang Prabang — once the royal capital — is the biggest draw and the country's capital, Vientiane, has its charms too, but the Laotian countryside is rarely explored by travellers.

Where there are visitors, there are facilities however, and Luang Prabang in particular caters for wealthy ones and backpackers alike.

Laos remains relatively unspoiled by the tourism industry thus far, and in the case of Luang Prabang at least, the typical Asian concrete development has been kept at bay.

Laos is not a destination for party animals, but that is also its charm. It is a peaceful and relaxed corner of a frenetic region.

Maison Souvannaphoum

If you were a royal, you would build your residence in the best location, no? That's the case with Maison Souvannaphoum, which is an easy walk to the historic centre of Luang Prabang (not that we imagine royalty taking that stroll), but also just far enough away to have plenty of space.

The hotel comprises the original residence, which dates back to the early 1960s, and a garden wing, which was built in the 1970s. After an extensive renovation, it re-opened its doors to guests in 2005.

Rooms in the Garden Wing are compact. So are the bathrooms, which feature bizarre fluorescent-orange plastic shower screens that belong in a Cantonese disco. All rooms in the Garden Wing have large private balconies that look out over the main house and the gardens, however.

In La Residence, each room is unique and all are larger than those in the Garden Wing, although only the Maison Suite has a balcony. We spent most of our time exploring the town, so the Garden Room was perfectly adequate. But if you're staying longer, choose the Maison Suite.

The charming dining area — Elephant Blanc — is open to the public and overlooks a small pool. It is one of the better restaurants in town, particularly for Lao cuisine.

Aside from a few minor décor disasters, Maison Souvannaphoum exudes charm. It's difficult not to love the place, which makes it the winner for us in Luang Prabang.

Maison Souvannaphoum Hotel

address   Rue Chao Fa Ngum,
          Banthatluang, PO Box 741,
          Luang Prabang, Lao PDR
phone   +856 71 254-609
web   www.coloursofangsana.com
capacity 24 rooms
rates   US$170-400++

Maison Souvannaphoum

ranking - lost weekend
The best of Luang Prabang.

luxe
• Peaceful • Comfortable • Quiet
• Excellent service

less luxe
• Strange décor touches • Small rooms in garden wing

best for
Relaxed atmosphere and facilities. Within walking distance of the historic centre of Luang Prabang.

✱ insider tip
For more space, upgrade to the Maison Suite — it is the only room in the old building with a balcony.

Settha Palace Hotel

In the sleepy capital of Laos, it is a genuine surprise to find an establishment quite as good as the Settha Palace. Of course you may find yourself wondering what you are doing in Vientiane — given the lack of high-profile attractions — but that is also what makes it so relaxed. There are things to see and do here but you probably won't need more than a long weekend to see it all.

The Settha Palace makes an ideal base for that couple of days though. While the hotel was renovated in the late 1990s, the owners resisted the temptation to cram in more rooms, so all the old charm remains.

Period features such as hardwood floors, high ceilings and French windows have been retained, though the rooms are a comfortable size rather than expansive. The smart, period-style bathrooms (with functional plumbing) have to be a rarity in Laos.

La Belle Epoque — the hotel's restaurant — offers fine French dining as well as Indian and Lao dishes.

The public areas feature marble floors and a massive light fixture in the lobby, and the hotel's friendly staff are always on-hand to fulfil any request.

We wish there were more hotels like this one. But there aren't — particularly in Vientiane — so booking ahead is essential. The Settha Palace Hotel is recognised as the best hotel in town, and deservedly so.

Settha Palace Hotel

address 6 Pang Kham Street, PO Box 1618, Vientiane, Lao PDR
phone +856 21 217-581/2
web www.setthapalace.com
capacity 29 rooms
rates US$180-380++

ranking - lost weekend
Small and smart. Central location and period charm. They don't get much better than this.

luxe
• Ambience • Service

less luxe
• Often booked out • Pool facilities are open to others on weekends

best for
Exploring Vientiane either by foot or in one of the hotel's London cabs.

✱ insider tip
For a more peaceful stay, ask for a room away from the pool.

Boutique Hotel Les 3 Nagas

The Boutique Hotel Les 3 Nagas is more of a guesthouse than a hotel and it has the advantage of being situated on Luang Prabang's main road. In fact, it has a building on either side of the main road. The lobby is in Lamache House, which offers several rooms upstairs like the one featured here, and a downstairs room too. Across the road is Villa Achan Thong Dy, which has a pleasant and peaceful garden and a more open feel.

There's no need to be too concerned about being on the main street: the traffic is fairly sparse and you can usually step out onto the road without too much fear. Try that in Bangkok.

The townsfolk wake early though, mainly to give alms to the Buddhist monks who live in the 45 temples in the immediate vicinity. This means morning is about the busiest time of day, but the flip side is a fairly peaceful time in the evenings.

The rooms are all different, and quirky, which reflects the fact that Boutique Hotel Les 3 Nagas was not designed as a hotel. Call it character. If you want a resort-style experience, you're in the wrong place, but Boutique Hotel Les 3 Nagas has plenty of charm nonetheless.

Boutique Hotel Les 3 Nagas

address   Sakkaline Road, Ban Vat Nong, PO Box 722, Luang Prabang, Lao PDR
phone   +856 71 253-888
web   www.3nagas.com
capacity 15 rooms
rates   US$85-180 (Seasonal)

Boutique Hotel Les 3 Nagas

ranking - one-night stand
A stylish guesthouse in the heart of Luang Prabang.

luxe
• Actually feels like you are in Laos

less luxe
• No pool

best for
Staying in the middle of the heritage-listed area.

✱ insider tip
Rooms in Villa Achan Thong Dy look out over a quiet garden.

La Résidence Phou Vao

ranking - one-night stand
The only purpose-built resort in Luang Prabang.

luxe
• Peaceful • Comfortable • Quiet

less luxe
• Décor that your parents would like
• Not within walking distance of town

best for
Kicking back by the pool after exploring Luang Prabang.

✱ insider tip
The rooms above the restaurant offer the best views.

Being situated on the outskirts of Luang Prabang is a blessing and a curse for La Résidence Phou Vao, which is part of the Pansea Orient-Express Hotels chain. The blessing is the peace it affords, despite being in a suburban area rather than the jungle; the curse is that the old part of Luang Prabang — the main reason to visit — is more than walking distance from the resort.

Still, if you want the nicest pool in Luang Prabang, it's at the Pansea, and the view of the temple in the distance always reminds you that you are a long way from Kansas.

And even if you do not bargain with the driver, a tuk-tuk ride to town will only set you back US$2 — or you could take the free shuttle.

The rooms are comfortable enough and purpose-built for the job, unlike most of the other hotels in town, which have typically been converted from another use, so the bottom-line is that at La Résidence Phou Vao you will be comfortable.

La Résidence Phou Vao

address	3 PO Box 50, Luang Prabang, Lao PDR
phone	+856 71 212-194
web	www.pansea.com
capacity	34 rooms
rates	US$240-400 (Seasonal)

Stay

Featured Hotels:
- Boutique Hotel Les 3 Nagas
- La Résidence Phou Vao
- Maison Souvannaphoum Hotel
- Settha Palace Hotel

Eat

JOMA BAKERY CAFÉ
+856 21 215-265
Setthathilat Road
Nam Phou Place
Vientiane, Lao PDR
Casual café-style dining that features home-made bread. Located right in the heart of town.

LA BELLE EPOQUE
+856 21 217-581/2
6 Pang Kham Street
Vientiane, Lao PDR
Another hotel restaurant — this time the Settha Palace — but easily the smartest restaurant in town.

ELEPHANT BLANC
+856 71 212-200
Rue Chao Fa Ngum
Banthatluang, PO Box 741
Luang Prabang, Lao PDR
The restaurant at Maison Souvannaphoum is worth a visit if you are not staying there. Don't miss the Lao specialities.

JOMA BAKERY CAFÉ
+856 71 252-292
Chao Fa Ngum Road
Luang Prabang, Lao PDR
Sister outlet to the one in Vientiane. The Luang Prabang outlet is not as close to the centre of town, but is in a charming colonial residence.

L'ELEPHANT RESTAURANT FRANÇAIS
+856 71 252-482
Ban Vat Nong
PO Box 812,
Luang Prabang, Lao PDR
A truly authentic French bistro that makes the most of local produce. If it wasn't for the passing monks and helpful waiting staff, you would think you were in Paris. An absolute must.

LEMONGRASS
+856 30 5140-092
BAN XIENG MOUAN
House01/11 St Sakalin
Luang Prabang, Lao PDR
A smart little (very little) wine bar on a quiet street overlooking the Mekong River. Who would have expected that?

See

TEMPLES
They are everywhere, some more compelling than others. In Luang Prabang, there are 45 to choose from. In Vientiane, the Sisaket Museum is captivating, with its numerous Buddha images and untouched main temple, which makes it the most interesting attraction in the capital.

CITYSCAPES
The best thing is to walk and explore in Luang Prabang and to a lesser degree in Vientiane. There is something interesting to see around every corner, from architecture, to temples, to Laotians leading their daily lives.

>>malaysia

Malaysia is overlooked by many travellers, but it does offer some surprises for those who love luxury.

In the capital, Kuala Lumpur, the trend is to build monumental buildings that too often verge on Las Vegas-style tackiness. But there is a thriving nightlife scene as well as some decent eateries.

On Peninsular Malaysia the west coast island of Langkawi has some stunning scenery and truly deluxe accommodation, while Penang offers a taste of colonial-era life.

The east coast islands boast some of the world's clearest tropical waters but there is very little in the way of upmarket tourist facilities. East Malaysia is a favourite for eco-travellers but currently lacks any truly individual accommodation options.

Malaysia is generally less chaotic than the rest of the South-East Asia and usually offers a warm welcome and some great food too.

The Datai

It is almost impossible to imagine a more stunning location for a resort than Datai Bay. An ancient rainforest meets the ocean at a perfect, crescent-shaped bay that is flanked by sheer mountains.

The Datai and a family-style resort are the only properties on the bay so unlike much of the rest of Asia, development has been well contained. Even the road from the small airport is so perfect that you would swear you were not in Asia at all, so long as you ignore the Disney-esque fake waterfall en route.

First impressions of the Datai are brilliant. The smooth check-in and attentive service are harbingers of more to come, and the treetop location is stunning — though the prices reflect this.

Most rooms are in the main building, which is divided into wings. Individual villas are located down the river valley, which leads to the sea. The upper floors in the main building have the best views out towards some neighbouring Thai islands, although noise from the poolside restaurant can intrude.

The rooms are comfortable and well-appointed, but the terraces are too small to be practical. The villas offer more outdoor space but are under the forest canopy, which is not the best for sun worshipers.

Great attention has been paid to lighting in the forest section between the main building and beach, making for a magical after-dinner walk. But remember: there are more than 100 steps back to the top.

The Datai

address	Jalan Teluk Datai, 07000 Pulau Langkawi, Kedah Darul Aman, Malaysia
phone	+60 4 959-2500
web	www.ghmhotels.com
capacity	112 rooms
rates	RM1,445-9,660 (Seasonal)

ranking - lost weekend
Arguably the best resort in Malaysia

luxe
• Location, location, location • Easy to get to • One of the two pools is designated child-free

less luxe
• Pricing • Not enough poolside space

best for
Enjoy the majesty of untouched nature without sacrificing luxury in any way.

✱ insider tip
The Datai Suite offers the best views as well as peace and quiet among the treetops.

Carcosa Seri Negara

Carcosa Seri Negara comprises two colonial buildings that date back to the early 20th century. The residences were built for British colonial chiefs and the genteel colonial ambience remains. You can even have high tea.

Of the two buildings, Carcosa gets the most attention, but when we visited it was looking a bit tired. We stayed in a large, comfortable suite in Seri Negara — a slightly less grand building that was built after Carcosa — and it seemed the best choice at the time.

The beauty of Carcosa Seri Negara is its size. With only 13 rooms, the service is exceptional and the atmosphere very relaxing and quiet, despite being just 10-minutes' drive from the centre of Kuala Lumpur.

But be warned: on the weekends there is an influx of people for the buffet lunch at Carcosa or high tea at Seri Negara. And being state-owned, local royalty (and there a lot of royals in Malaysia) treat it as their own, which can't be a good thing for paying guests. Under the new management of GHM, some of these pitfalls may have been fixed.

Carcosa Seri Negara
address   Taman Tasik Perdana,
           Persiaran Mahameru,
           50480 Kuala Lumpur, Malaysia
phone   +60 3 2295-0888
web   www.ghmhotels.com
capacity   13 rooms
rates   RM1,100-3,500++

ranking - lost weekend

Colonial grandeur close to the heart of town.

luxe

• Victorian/Edwardian period ambience
• Small and friendly

less luxe

• Carcosa needs restoration as does the pool area • Pricing

best for

High tea overlooking the garden and Kuala Lumpur skyline.

✳ insider tip

Seri Negara is not as grand as Carcosa, but it is quieter.

Cheong Fatt Tze Mansion

Cheong Fatt Tze Mansion could be from another part of the world. Regular visitors to Italy will be familiar with the owner-hosted stay in a *pensione*, but in Asia most equivalents met the blade of a bulldozer long ago.

Cheong Fatt Tze is a privately owned mansion that has been painstakingly restored to its former glory using traditional techniques. People who know Asia will realise just how rare this approach is compared with the usual concrete-everything-in-sight philosophy.

Each room has a unique charm, although if you don't like traditional Chinese style most will not appeal. We stayed in the quirky Old Kitchen, decorated with period cookware and with its original stove in place.

With only 16 rooms, Cheong Fatt Tze Mansion is more a bed-and-breakfast than a full-service hotel, so don't expect facilities such as pools, but do expect a personal approach that is rare.

The mansion is located in the middle of the historic district in Penang, meaning local colour is simply a short walk away. There are daily public tours of the building, which are well worth joining just to put things in context, although they do mean a daily incursion by the general public. At least the tours do not last long and are not too intrusive.

But don't just take our word about how good Cheong Fatt Tze Mansion is. It was used as a location for the movie *Indochine* starring Catherine Deneuve — need we say more?

Cheong Fatt Tze Mansion

address 14 Leith Street, 10200 Penang, Malaysia
phone   +60 4 262-0006
web   www.cheongfatttze mansion.com
capacity 15 rooms
rates   RM250-700

ranking - lost weekend

This is a unique property. If you like Georgetown (and many don't), you will never want to leave.

luxe

• Quirky rooms • Feeling of exclusivity at a reasonable price

less luxe

• No facilities — sooner or later in the tropics a pool is a good thing

best for

Exploring Georgetown by foot and experiencing life as it might have been if you were a Mandarin.

* insider tip

The rooms have different themes. If you don't like dark furniture or an intensely Chinese ambience, you might want a room like the Old Kitchen with more neutral tones.

Eastern & Oriental Hotel Penang

Established by the Sarkies brothers at about the same time they built the Raffles in Singapore, the Eastern & Oriental Hotel has hardly achieved Raffles' fame. Blame geography.

This is not such a bad thing for visitors. The E&O offers much the same colonial ambience as Raffles but at less than half the price. Also the E&O wins with its waterside location, something Raffles lost long ago after extensive land reclamation in Singapore.

But comparing a stay at the E&O with Raffles is like comparing chalk to cheese. Raffles is an anomaly in glossy Singapore, whereas the E&O fits right in with the largely untouched historic centre of Georgetown.

The recent restoration of the hotel has bizarrely seen many of its original antique pieces shipped off to its sister beach resort, The Lone Pine, replaced by reproduction antique furniture that looks like reproduction antique furniture.

As a general rule it's not drastically bad but the light fitting in our bedroom was straight out of a *Brady Bunch* episode. What were they thinking? The occasional Laura Ashley touch can be a bit too much for some tastes as well.

Odd furnishings aside, at the E&O you can expect friendly service, a great location, well-proportioned rooms, and an ideal base from which to explore Georgetown, which is unlike anywhere else in South-East Asia.

If you feel like splurging, some of the Writer's Suites have original, clawfoot bathtubs in the well-appointed bathrooms. All but 12 of the 101 suites face the water, with uninterrupted views across the straits and the sunset when there is one, and the standard Deluxe Suite actually does fulfil the promise of its name.

You will probably feel like dressing for dinner.

Eastern & Oriental Hotel Penang

address	10 Lebuh Farquhar, 10200 Penang, Malaysia
phone	+60 4 222-2000
web	www.e-o-hotel.com
capacity	101 rooms
rates	RM750-12,000+++

Eastern & Oriental Hotel Penang

ranking - lost weekend
Colonial splendour in a historic city.

luxe
• Historic atmosphere • Water views
• Large rooms

less luxe
• Penang is not the world's most happening city in terms of nightlife
• Reproduction antiques • No beach

best for
A stopover to explore one of the more historically interesting cities in the region.

* insider tip
Many rooms on the first floor have small balconies.

Tanjong Jara

Tanjong Jara is a sister resort of the much better-known Pangkor Laut, but it is not necessarily a poorer cousin.

Situated an hour's drive south of Kuala Terengganu — the nearest big town and airport — Tanjong Jara does not get many casual drop-ins. If you stay in the off-season, you will probably have one of the two pools completely to yourself, though the beach is not the best at that time of year.

Of the three main room options, the Anjung is the pick mainly because of the extra space it affords, although the décor is a bit dated. The outdoor bathtub and pleasant balcony make it worth the extra money, however.

As befits a resort of this size and quality, there is a choice of two restaurants and room service. It also has a spa and the funkiest little gym you are ever likely to see, with glass walls under a traditional Malay-style roof.

Tanjong Jara is not the choice if you want to be in the middle of the action — tranquillity is the main attraction here. Seasonal watersports activities including diving and snorkelling trips to nearby islands. Diving courses can be arranged and equipment can be rented at the resort.

There are various activities away from the resort such as visits to local night markets and jungle treks, but if you are looking for the hottest clubs in Terengganu, you are in the wrong place — there aren't any.

For a peaceful, restful and quiet holiday though you could do much worse than Tanjong Jara.

Tanjong Jara Resort

address   Batu 8, off Jalan Dungun, 23000 Dungun, Terengganu, Malaysia
phone   +60 9 845-1100
web   www.tanjongjararesort.com
capacity 99 rooms
rates   RM805-2,415

Natural
Crystals from
the Dead Sea

In a soothing, relaxing
refreshing experience,
you are invited to soak in
a naturally scented warm bath!
The powers of the
natural minerals provided
by these Crystals help to
relieve aches and pains,
prevent stiffness after
exercise, relax the muscles,
dissipate tension around
the neck and back, and
alleviate stress and
headache.
The container is suitable for two baths.

ranking - lost weekend
A modern full-service resort, with some traditional Malay architecture and furnishings.

luxe
• Quaint setting along a river valley
• Big stretch of private beach

less luxe
• The beach is not pleasant during the monsoon season between November and March • Maintenance could be better • Prices are high

best for
Thoroughly quiet escape from the modern world.

✱ insider tip
The Anjung suite (pictured) is the best.

The Aryani

The tiny, 20-room, family owned and run Aryani is a rare gem in this part of the world. The east coast of peninsular Malaysia can be pretty, but along the 1,000 kilometres or so of coast there are only the two resorts that are not the large, concrete, hideously ugly mass-tourism hotels that are so common here.

Our deluxe room was comfortable, with a giant bed and neat little outdoor bath. However, the proximity to neighbouring rooms and low walls made us avoid using the bathtub. The indoor bathroom is stylish but the fittings could be improved, likewise the cane chairs in the bedroom seemed out of place with the otherwise stylish look.

The Modern Suite offers a little more style and has a bathtub in the room behind the bedhead, as well as better ocean views. But for our money the best choice is the Redang suite, which is a 140-year-old traditional Malay house transplanted to this beachfront setting. Its rustic style might not appeal to everyone — the main sitting room does get dark because of the wood panelling and so few windows — but the experience is unique.

The resort is small and you are unlikely to be crowded by other guests even though the pool is compact, but we think it would have been better if the rooms had a little more distance between them anyway.

Be aware of the monsoon from November to March: there is not necessarily constant torrential rain, but access to marine activities such as swimming at the beach and visiting the islands just off the coast is restricted.

The accommodation is not the ultimate in luxury, but the quiet location, the unique Redang suite and some good package deals make it an intriguing choice.

The Aryani

address	Jalan Rhu Tapai-Merang, 21010 Setiu, Terengganu, Malaysia
phone	+60 9 653-2111
web	www.thearyani.com
capacity	20 rooms
rates	RM308-1,055

ranking - one-night stand

Quiet, peaceful, restful, with a choice of modern or traditional Malay-style accommodation.

luxe

- Peace and quiet • Imaginative food
- Relaxing • Small

less luxe

- No alcohol when we visited, though there is an outlet for non-Muslims now
- In the middle of nowhere

best for

Lock yourself away, have a spa treatment and escape from the world for a few days.

✱ insider tip

The Redang suite is unique, but can be a bit dark indoors, otherwise the Modern Suite is the choice.

Stay

Featured Hotels:
- The Aryani
- Carcosa Seri Negara
- Cheong Fatt Tze Mansion
- The Datai
- Eastern & Oriental Hotel Penang
- Tanjong Jara Resort

Also:

MANDARIN ORIENTAL, KUALA LUMPUR
+60 3 2380-8888
Kuala Lumpur City Centre
50088 Kuala Lumpur
Malaysia
www.mandarin-oriental.com
The address says it all. Right next to the Petronas Twin Towers (yesterday the world's tallest buildings; today, the tallest twin towers — but impressive anyway), and home to a decent shopping mall with a wide selection of food outlets.

THE WESTIN, KUALA LUMPUR
+60 3 2731-8333
199 Jalan Bukit Bintang
55100 Kuala Lumpur
Malaysia
www.westin.com
Its location on Kuala Lumpur's most famous shopping district (Bukit Bintang) and attractive design make the Westin a good choice. The advertised 'heavenly beds' really are heavenly and powerful water pressure makes showering heavenly too.

HOTEL MAYA
+60 3 2711-8866
138 Jalan Ampang
50450 Kuala Lumpur
Malaysia
www.hotelmaya.com.my
Funky rooms and a guests-only bar that looks out over the Petronas Twin Towers should make Hotel Maya a must-stay, but the building is too big and impersonal for a truly boutique experience.

Eat

Malaysia, like Singapore, is one of the few places in the region where the food from street vendors is safe. In Kuala Lumpur, veer off Jalan Bukit Bintang and head for Jalan Alor where an entire road almost closes down for the evening.

Prices are low enough that you can try just about anything. Likewise in Penang, the Gurney Drive hawker centre is brilliant — try an Assam Laksa for only RM2 if you are ready for some spice. Brilliant.

In Kuala Lumpur if you're admiring the Twin Towers after dark there are a number of reasonable offerings in KLCC overlooking the park and fountain. They're mostly casual pizza and pasta places and mostly pretty good too. Take your pick.

ATRIUM
+60 3 2694-1318
Asian Heritage Row, 21 Jalan Doraisamy
Kuala Lumpur, Malaysia

Don't let the Asian Heritage Row address put you off: this is not a contrived tourist-trap. Atrium offers contemporary cuisine in a contemporary setting, and a choice of bars for an after-dinner drink or two.

EEST
+60 3 2731-8333
The Westin, Kuala Lumpur
199 Jalan Bukit Bintang,
55100 Kuala Lumpur, Malaysia

Eest is a hotel restaurant, but worth a visit in any case. The name should give the game away when it comes to cuisine, with a range of choices from across Asia, and the modern, airy interior is at the cutting-edge of hotel chic.

See

EAST MALAYSIA

Tourist attractions in Malaysia are a bit sparse. East Malaysia is the place to go for natural attractions: unspoiled rainforests, incredibly beautiful marine parks and orang-utan sanctuaries. But don't expect small, quirky or funky accommodation.

KUALA LUMPUR

Peninsular Malaysia offers some impressive natural scenery too, particularly on the east coast, but the cities are the places to go. In Kuala Lumpur, the colonial architecture is impressive and at Merdeka Square you are in the heart of it. We were not particularly impressed by their "world's biggest" titles, but the Petronas Twin Towers are worth seeing, particularly after dark.

CENTRAL MARKET

If you have not experienced a typical Asian night market, then you should visit the Central Market, which has its stock of fake designer handbags and pirated DVDs at vastly inflated asking prices (the mainstay of just about every Asian night market, it seems).

>>singapore

Straight-laced and sterile are not kind descriptions of tightly controlled Singapore, but there is some truth in them. In other South-East Asian cities, you expect traffic chaos and a certain amount of grime and squalor, but Singapore is different.

The tiny island-nation may seem dull to many experienced Asia travellers, but the cleanliness can be a bonus for first-time visitors to the region. Even experienced travellers must have at least some admiration for the ruthlessly efficient airport.

But you only need to scratch the surface to find that Singapore is letting its hair down a little. There is a thriving and often vibrant bar and restaurant scene, and the varied local food with its Chinese, Malay, and Indian influences is fantastic. All this makes Singapore a worthy stopover destination.

Raffles Hotel

One of the standard tourist activities in Singapore is to drink a Singapore Sling in the Long Bar at Raffles. It is such a common request that the bar staff keep a pre-mixed supply of the sweet concoction ready to go.

But don't make the mistake of believing that a stay at Raffles means fighting through throngs of visitors at every turn. Public access to the residential part of the hotel is restricted, which results in an extraordinarily peaceful stay.

Raffles is an obvious choice in Singapore — with good reason. It is internationally known but is still a relatively small hotel with just 103 suites. The restoration of the hotel, completed in 1991, was done with great sympathy for the original building.

Rooms feature hardwood floors and 14-foot ceilings, and are furnished to reflect the hotel's heyday during the First World War. More than 400 pieces of original antique furniture and details such as period-style brass light switches are a nice touch. However, Raffles is not the place to stay if century-old style does not ring your bell.

The two-bedroom presidential suites are enormous, lavishly furnished and outrageously expensive. The standard suites offer a small sitting/dining area, leading to the bedroom. Ten suites are themed and decorated with memorabilia connected with the many authors who have called Raffles home over the years.

You pay handsomely for it, but a stay at Raffles is truly memorable.

Raffles Hotel

address	1 Beach Road, Singapore 189673
phone	+65 6337-1886
web	www.raffleshotel.com
capacity	103 rooms
rates	S$800-4,000+++

111

ranking - lifetime love

If it weren't for the berserk credit card bill, we would find a reason to extend.

luxe

• Quiet period ambience • Privacy in the residential areas • Lush greenery • Close to shops and the colonial district

less luxe

• Can feel a bit stuffy at times • Pool area is disappointing

best for

Recreating the colonial lifestyle.

✳ insider tip

If you are fabulously wealthy, take the palatial Grand Hotel Suite, but for everyone else a Courtyard Suite is fine.

New Majestic Hotel

Experience is a great teacher and that is obvious at the New Majestic, which has the same owners as Hotel 1929 (just around the corner). The recently opened New Majestic has much larger rooms and more breathing space in the public areas than Hotel 1929. There is even a pool.

Design is central to the New Majestic, which is fine, but it does come across as being a bit forced. At times, there are too many elements fighting for attention. The design arguably works better in the guest rooms than the public areas. The rooms were handed over to local artists for individual treatment, but this means some will be to your tastes and others not. While one looks like a Las Vegas bordello, an identical room just down the hall is slick, modern and white.

Choose carefully.

The pool area is smart enough, although there is only space for about eight people on the deck around it. Several glass portholes over the restaurant below mean you could cause some consternation if you choose to adjust your swimming attire at the wrong moment. It would be nice if they provided towels by the pool — a symptom of the style-first, practicality-later nature of the place.

Still, of the newcomers to the Singapore boutique hotel scene, the New Majestic is arguably the best.

New Majestic Hotel

address	31-37 Bukit Pasoh Road Singapore 089845
phone	+65 6511-4700
web	www.newmajestichotel.com
capacity	30 rooms
rates	S$280-600+++

singapore > stay
New Majestic Hotel

ranking - lost weekend
Every room is unique.

luxe
• Great location • Funky

less luxe
• Laclustre service • Breakfast is appalling

best for
A uniquely Singapore experience.

✱ insider tip
The top-floor suites have almost no natural light; balcony rooms at the front of the hotel are the best.

The Scarlet

Singapore is replete with five-star international chain hotels, but good boutique accommodation is rare. Only in the past few years has that niche opened up on the island, which is odd for a city that promotes itself as a modern, cosmopolitan metropolis. But that means the boutique places are new — and it shows at times.

The rooms at The Scarlet are smart enough, but we recommend going for the more expensive ones with natural light. The suites are where The Scarlet really shines. With names such as Splendour, Passion, Opulent, Lavish, and Swank, you get some idea of the design ethos.

In our experience the service needs attention, however. There is more to hospitality than just a smart building, and all the boutique places in Singapore apart from Raffles have yet to figure this out. Maybe they will with time.

But in a country filled with homogenous hotels, The Scarlet is ostentatiously stylish, which has to be a good thing. If you want individuality, The Scarlet has it in abundance.

The Scarlet

address	33 Erskine Road, Singapore 069333
phone	+65 6511-3333
web	www.thescarlethotel.com
capacity	84 rooms
rates	S$220-800+++

ranking - one-night stand
All style.

luxe
• Great location • Plush interior design

less luxe
• Little outdoor space • Service could be improved • Pricing

best for
Exploring Chinatown and its trendier eating and drinking establishments.

✱ insider tip
The lower-cost rooms do not have windows, so lash out on a room with a balcony.

123

Hotel 1929

Hotel 1929 occupies a row of shophouses built in 1929 — hence the name — and is located on Keong Saik Road, which is better known by locals as a designated red-light district. In any other city this might mean sleaze and crime but not in Singapore. Unless you mistake one of the nearby houses (identified only by a large street number) for a shop, there is very little chance you will notice the flesh pedalling going on nearby.

The hotel offers a trendy fusion dining experience in restaurant Ember downstairs, but you are just as likely to enjoy any of the local coffee shops for an extraordinarily cheap lunch or dinner.

The rooms at Hotel 1929 add a new dimension to the notion of compact — there is not enough space to swing a kitten, let alone a cat — but the designers have done everything possible to make the rooms functional. A safe in the drawer under the bed is an efficient use of minimal space, although the toilet in the shower cubicle will not make every guest happy.

We suggest taking one of the suites, which are equipped with en suite bathrooms as well as outside showers, even if the latter are not as private as you might expect.

Hotel 1929

address	150 Keong Saik Road, Singapore 089154
phone	+65 6347-1929
web	www.hotel1929.com
capacity	32 rooms
rates	S$120-280+++

ranking - one-night stand

A good place for a short stopover in Singapore.

luxe

• Groovy design • Cool restaurant
• Cosy ambience amid local colour

less luxe

• Smallest rooms this side of a filing cabinet • No pool • No room service

best for

A short stay with a taste of local life.

✱ insider tip

Take the suite with rooftop garden and shower — it is less claustrophobic.

Stay

Featured Hotels:
- Hotel 1929
- The New Majestic
- Raffles Hotel
- The Scarlet

Also:

FOUR SEASONS SINGAPORE
+65 6734-1110
190 Orchard Boulevard
Singapore 248646
www.fourseasons.com
Beds that guests rave about (they are actually for sale), slick service and close to the Orchard shopping strip.

GRAND HYATT
+65 6738-1234
10 Scotts Road,
Singapore 228211
www.hyatt.com
The newly renovated rooms are a surprise — they are actually stylish! Good location and great food and beverages, although it comes at a price.

RITZ CARLTON, MILLENIA SINGAPORE
+65 6337-8888
7 Raffles Avenue
Singapore 039799
www.ritzcarlton.com
For a bathtub with a view, the Ritz Carlton cannot be beaten, but the Marina district location is pretty sterile.

SINGAPORE MARRIOTT HOTEL
+65 6735-5800
320 Orchard Road
Singapore 238865
www.marriott.com
Arguably the best address in Singapore, particularly if you are there to shop. The new Pool Terrace rooms offer a taste of resort-style living in the heart of town.

Eat

"Have you eaten" is a more common Singapore greeting than "How are you", which gives some indication of the importance of food in the culture. The array of choices and extremes of cost are quite amazing.

Local favourites such as Hainanese chicken rice, spicy *laksa* soup, and fried *kway teow* noodles can be found in just about every food court and the many corner coffee shops around the island. If you are in a shopping mall at lunchtime, head for the basement where there is always a good chance of finding a food court. Do not be afraid of the many open-air coffee shops. Hygiene standards are fine and the food is extraordinarily cheap. Try the Geylang area (another red-light district) for a fantastic choice — just about every cabbie will suggest a favourite. But be warned: most of the favourite dishes are loaded with saturated fats.

NEWTON FOOD CENTRE
Corner of Bukit Timah Road and Clemenceau Avenue
Newton Circus is justly famous as an outdoor food centre. Sitting under the trees in the evening is pleasant, but Newton is also a tourist trap. We suggest that you agree on a price before ordering. Newton has recently been renovated but just why is beyond us. Who knows what the shiny new Newton will be like — hopefully some of the charm will remain.

MARMALADE PANTRY
+65 6734-2700
390 Orchard B108-11
Palais Renaissance, Singapore

Marmalade Pantry might be one of the trendier lunch stops in Orchard road, although you would never guess it from its basement location. Great juice blends and the best steak sandwich anywhere make it a winner, but it is best to book in advance.

MEZZA9
+65 6738-1234
Grand Hyatt
10 Scotts Road, Singapore

Many of the bigger hotels put on an excellent Sunday brunch, most offering a free-flow of Champagne as well. Hyatt's mezza9 offers an almost too-slick atmosphere, excellent buffet food and a never-ending glass of bubbly.

PIERSIDE KITCHEN
+65 6438-0400
1 Fullerton Road
Fullerton One, Singapore

A stylish little restaurant right on the waterfront at Fullerton One, Pierside Kitchen's decent menu and wine list come at fairly reasonable prices for Singapore. Try the miso cod — it is a winner.

PROJECT SHOP CAFÉ
+65 6735-6765
290 Orchard Road
#03-41 Paragon, Singapore

One of the funkier lunchtime stopovers in the busy Orchard Road shopping strip. Daily specials on blackboards and good cakes make it a worthwhile stop, even if service is erratic and it is difficult to get a table.

SAMY'S CURRY RESTAURANT
+65 6472-2080
Block 25
Dempsey Road, Singapore

A Singapore institution. Samy's is housed in a not particularly charming colonial dining hall, but surrounded by lush greenery. Expect excellent Indian food dished up on banana leaves and low prices.

See

NIGHT SAFARI

Singapore's best tourist attraction is the Night Safari — and yes, it is a zoo. Take the train that winds slowly through the jungle or wander along the walking path on a balmy tropical night and see the animals while they are actually awake. It is a bit of a trek to get there but well worth the effort.

LITTLE INDIA

Little India is only ten minutes from Orchard but a world away. Step out of the cab in to what seems like a different country, which so far has been largely — and mercifully — spared from the relentless bulldozers and concrete modernity that characterises the rest of the Singapore. Get to Little India for wildly colourful shops, aromatic spice stalls and great low-cost food.

129

>>thailand

While travelling around Thailand, particularly in gridlocked Bangkok, it will occur that there are more luxurious pastimes, but Thailand makes up its faults with the friendliness of its people, sensational food, stunning scenery, and some of the hippest hotels and shops in the region. In fact Bangkok is the capital of cool in South-East Asia.

The optimism in Thailand is infectious. The place is leaping ahead and whether you are lying on a beach, maxing out your credit cards shopping, or enjoying a cultural experience, you can feel the energy.

With brilliant beaches, fabulous food, extraordinary spas, buzzing Bangkok, great shopping, and even cool countryside breaks, the country has it all.

If you can't find anything to love about Thailand, get your doctor to make sure you still have a pulse.

Sila Evason Hideaway at Samui

When the Evason group says hideaway, it means hideaway. The Sila Evason Hideaway at Samui is on a quiet peninsula on the northern tip of Koh Samui, occupying an entire headland.

There is a pleasant beach at the eastern side of the resort although you have to negotiate a fairly steep path to get there. But why bother when there is a pool in your villa compound as well as a fantastic main pool on top of the hill?

You probably will not want to drag yourself away from your villa at all. The rooms have views out over the ocean, plenty of areas to sit and read a book, and enormous bathrooms, some with views from the bathtub.

Our room had views to the east and the west from the glass-enclosed bedroom, so it was possible to laze around in bed and admire the scenery, though the pool in the villa was much more of an attraction. It was a shame that our neighbours could see in.

The rustic décor is just like that at other Six Senses resorts, so you could experience Evason fatigue if you have been to a few. If not, some of the details are surprisingly imaginative.

The Thai food here is brilliant — not watered-down for western palates — and the breakfast buffet sets the standards that others need to follow.

Easily the best resort on the island of Koh Samui.

Sila Evason Hideaway at Samui

address 9/10 Moo 5, Baan Plai Laem, Bophut, Koh Samui, Surathani 84320, Thailand
phone +66 77 245-678
web www.six-senses.com
capacity 66 rooms
rates THB15,970-131,470+++ (Seasonal)

133

ranking - lifetime love
Great villas. Great service. Great location.

luxe
• Spacious rooms • Service extras
• Brilliant Thai food

less luxe
• Disappointing Western food
• Less-than-private villa pools

best for
Locking yourself away in rustic luxury.

✱ insider tip
Make the effort to use the main pool
— it is worth it.

Sukhothai

It is difficult to know where to start and where to stop singing the praises of The Sukhothai. Leave the berserk Bangkok traffic on South Sathorn Road behind, and enter the far more gracious world of the Sukhothai. In the stylish foyer, a centrepiece of fresh tuberoses offers up an intoxicating and welcoming scent.

The rooms feature muted gold silks and the mirrored, wood-panelled bathrooms are brilliant, though it pays to upgrade rooms if you are a bathroom fanatic, as they are substantially smaller in the basic rooms.

Guest rooms are spread over two wings, so the hotel never quite feels as large as the total number of rooms would suggest. Subtle landscaping and architectural details add to the atmosphere of peace and privacy. The many open courtyards and long colonnaded walkways offer tantalising glimpses of water features or traditional Thai artefacts.

This is a full-service hotel with all the amenities you would expect at an international standard hotel, but with a much warmer, more welcoming feel. Even business travellers are well looked-after with high-speed internet connections.

As with everything else, eating is a pleasure at The Sukhothai, with an indulgent breakfast buffet and the renowned Celadon Thai restaurant, which is worth a visit even for those not in residence.

Absolutely a winner.

The Sukhothai

address	13/3 South Sathorn Road Bangkok 10120, Thailand
phone	+66 2 344-8888
web	www.sukhothai.com
capacity	210 rooms
rates	US$290-2,100++

ranking - lifetime love
Do we really have to leave?

luxe
• Slick design • Brilliant service • Utter serenity in the midst of a frenetic city

less luxe
• Situated on a ridiculously busy eight-lane road — if you must leave the hotel compound • Sweaty walk to the SkyTrain

best for
Total luxury and a feeling of exclusivity in a city setting.

✳ insider tip
Upgrade to an executive suite for loads of room and brilliant bathrooms at only a small premium.

143

Rayavadee

You can't help but be overwhelmed by the stunning scenery on arrival at Rayavadee, and better still, the boat drops you off at the most disappointing of the three Rayavadee beach frontages. The other two are even more spectacular.

If you wrote a wish list of natural features to build a resort around, you could not do better than this.

Rayavadee's individual villas dot a coconut plantation that is dwarfed by massive jungle-clad limestone formations. Phra Nang Beach in particular is breathtaking and probably the most photographed beach in Thailand.

The downside is that easy boat access from Ao Nang means the beach is often overwhelmed by day-trippers. The resort handles this well by providing private decks overlooking the sand and keeping the general public out.

Architecturally, the villas are a bit of a concern, dotting the landscape like a bunch of giant mushrooms. But they are functional, comfortable and difficult to leave when the time comes. However, the swinging bathroom doors and so-so water pressure could be fixed.

Another quibble: the Thai meal we tried was a little disappointing.

Overall, though, it is hard to fault Rayavadee. From the smooth transfers, to the welcoming service, to the seemingly endless touches to make you feel welcome, Rayavadee fulfils its promise. The stunning location is a bonus.

Rayavadee

address	214 Moo 2, Tambol Ao-Nang Amphur Muang, Krabi 81000, Thailand
phone	+66 75 620-740
web	www.rayavadee.com
capacity	103 rooms
rates	US$462-1,897++ (Seasonal)

thailand > stay
Rayavadee

ranking - lifetime love
If you are alive and breathing, this place will impress you.

luxe
• Spacious and quiet rooms • Stunning scenery • Loads of extras included such as spa goodies in the bathroom and proper coffee facilities in the room

less luxe
• The pool is showing its age • Décor will not please all tastes

best for
Lazing around on one of the world's most spectacular beaches and watching the sun go down from the extraordinary Grotto Bar.

✱ insider tip
Spa and Hydro Pool Pavilions offer more private outdoor areas than the Deluxe Pavilions.

Costa Lanta

The sleek, sparse, unadorned bungalows at Costa Lanta mark a dramatic departure from the usual Thai resort. Twenty polished-concrete and unfinished wood structures dot the rear of Costa Lanta's large beachfront plot. Most have walls that open to allow the sea breeze into the bedroom with its mosquito-netted double bed.

A waterway snakes through the property, crossed by footbridges that give access to the beach, restaurant and pool. Unfortunately, the water can get stagnant at certain times of the year.

The design is the main attraction here, although sometimes style takes priority over substance. The big doors on the standard rooms can be hard to open and close, and it feels like you are sleeping in a garage with the doors closed. For this reason, we would choose one of the four more user-friendly superior rooms.

The rooms are architecturally attractive, but the lofty restaurant and bar is the focus of the resort. Subdued lounge music sets the scene, without drowning out the lapping of waves. The Thai food is excellent, although the service is often at a slow island pace. Massive doors are permanently open for the cooling sea breezes.

With only 22 rooms and a large block,

you never feel crowded at Costa Lanta, although more vegetation between the rooms would add to the privacy. The giant new resort being built next door could affect the relative peace of Costa Lanta, but it is difficult guess how much.

For the style conscious, Costa Lanta stands alone: way too cool.

Costa Lanta

address	212 Moo 1, Saladan, Amphur Koh Lanta, Krabi, Thailand
phone	+66 75 684-630/2
web	www.costalanta.com
capacity	22 rooms
rates	THB3,025-10,780 (seasonal)

ranking - lost weekend

At times, too groovy for its own good but unlike anything else you will find.

luxe

• Slick design • Cool pool • Right on a pretty beach • Few guests makes for tranquillity • Not very child friendly • More sun-loungers than guests

less luxe

• A long-haul trip from anywhere and there are no genuinely luxe ways to get there
• Tap water can smell awful — and you will be showering in it • High prices at peak times

best for

Chilling out in style.

✱ insider tip

Take a superior room for a more comfortable experience.

155

The Racha

If you want to get away from it all, The Racha is willing to oblige. Getting there can be a bit of a chore — particularly if the weather is rough — as it is on Koh Racha Yai, an island 20 kilometres south of Phuket. You could spend an hour on a speedboat bobbing around like a cork. We did.

But the location could not be prettier — on a well-protected bay that is popular with divers and snorkellers. The white walls of the Racha contrast starkly with the stunning blue sky, green foliage, and aquamarine water.

It is not all roses in paradise: the rooms could be more private and the service was friendly but a bit lacklustre during our visit (although the resort had just reopened after the tsunami, so it may have improved); the lights were so unfathomable that we ended up leaving them on in the sitting room of our pool villa; and the quality of the food needs improvement — particularly breakfast.

Fortunately, there are backpacker places nearby, so you are not stuck with resort food if you don't want it (at least during the peak season), and the place is awfully pretty.

The Racha scores points for style though, and if some of the little niggles could be fixed, it would be one of the better destination hotels in Thailand.

The Racha

address	42/12-13 Moo 5 Rawai, Muang Phuket 83130, Thailand
phone	+ 66 76 355-455
web	www.theracha.com
capacity	70 rooms
rates	US$250-1,300 (Seasonal)

The Racha

ranking - lost weekend
Superb beach and stylish villas.
Almost perfect.

luxe
• Location • Style

less luxe
• Transfer can be rough • Needs more substance to go with the style, particularly with service and food

best for
Getting away from Phuket.

✷ insider tip
Beachfront villas are the best by a fair margin.

Aleenta

Boutique is possibly the most overused word in the hotel marketers' jargon — but with only seventeen rooms, Aleenta Resort and Spa can truly lay claim to the word.

Five rooms are on the retaining wall on the beach, and of these, the Pool Villas are our pick although none are as private as you might like. Five more rooms are housed in a three-storey structure behind the single-storey Pool Villas, offering sea views from the second-floor rooms and penthouse above.

Pak Nam Pran beach is not one of Thailand's prettiest beaches, but it is quiet, so if you want a relatively undisturbed time, Aleenta might just be the right place. Unfortunately, it is a long three- to four-hour drive from Bangkok, making it difficult to get to.

Being located right on the shoreline makes maintenance an issue, but it does mean peace and quiet given the almost deserted beach. Don't expect to discover much local colour here — there is very little to see within walking distance.

Small bathrooms and a lack of wardrobe space aside, Aleenta gets just about everything right. If you want to get away from Bangkok for a weekend escape, it is one of the better choices.

**Aleenta Resort and Spa,
Hua Hin Pranburi**

address   183 Moo 4, Paknampran,
          Pranburi, Prachuabkirikhan
          77220, Thailand
phone   +66 2 508-5333
web   www.aleenta.com
capacity 17 rooms
rates   THB4,950-17,500++ (Seasonal)

ranking - lost weekend
Only ten rooms in the main hotel and no children under 12 — a policy for true serenity.

luxe
• The welcoming and personal service you can only get in a place this small

less luxe
• Not the greatest beach in Thailand
• Bathrooms are too small

best for
Listen to the waves lapping the shore while digesting a good book.

✳ insider tip
Go for a Pool Villa with uninterrupted water views and its own outdoor spa pool.

Twinpalms Phuket

At first sight, we thought Twinpalms was another of those too-cool properties that are more about style than substance. A resort hotel in Phuket that is not on the beach? Surely they jest.

But Twinpalms makes up for its location in several ways. First, it is only a two-minute walk from Surin Beach — one of the prettiest and least spoiled on the island. (Be sure to have a meal at one of the beachside shacks — it is one of the highlights of Phuket.)

Second, it backs that style up with substance: service standards are high and there is great attention to detail, with well-stocked mini bars, big towels (and lots of them), tasteful toiletries, and good quality bedding.

The rooms are quite small and too close together for completely secluded privacy, but Twinpalms is well worth considering if Phuket is your destination.

ranking - one-night stand
A small, funky hotel in Phuket without painful pricing — wonders will never cease.

luxe
• Great beach with brilliant local restaurants almost on the doorstep
• Surprising bathrooms • Luxury touches

less luxe
• Not close enough to the beach for sea views or the sound of the waves

best for
A stylish taste of Phuket.

Twinpalms Phuket
address	106/46 Moo 3 Surin Beach Road Cherng Talay, Thalang Phuket 83110, Thailand
phone	+ 66 76 316-500
web	www.twinpalms-phuket.com
capacity	76 rooms
rates	US$130-1,450 (Seasonal)

✳ insider tip
Oriental Spoon is one of the hottest restaurants on the island — you may need to book ahead, particularly for Sunday brunch.

Four Seasons Resort Chiang Mai

Until recently, the Four Seasons Resort Chiang Mai had a monopoly on high-end accommodation in northern Thailand. If you want polished luxury in the north, this has it.

What this does not mean is that Four Seasons is complacent. The extra 10 per cent that separates the good from the great seems to be what it strives for — but you pay handsomely for the privilege.

Clustered in groups of four, 64 Lanna-style Pavilion Rooms surround a terraced valley that the hotel uses to cultivate rice. The two-storey duplex buildings offer salas for each room along short walkways, although they are not quite as private as we would like.

The rooms are tasteful, but the décor does give away its 1995 origins, with woodwork that just looks very 1990s. Still,

it didn't seem that anything was falling apart or looking tatty during our visit.

On the opposite side of the valley from the rooms are the three-storey Residences, offering guests the choice of the ground floor, with it's own plunge pool, or the upper two floors, which are three-bedroom penthouse suites.

These massive suites are brilliant for a group, although drawing straws for the rooms in the penthouse will be entertaining — one of the three main rooms is a twin. Each residence features a fireplace for any cold winter nights and a live-in housekeeper.

The Four Seasons Resort Chiang Mai has a selection of food and beverage outlets and a stylish spa. If you really must do something, there is a cooking school to keep you busy too.

Four Seasons Resort Chiang Mai

address	Mae Rim-Samoeng Old Road, Mae Rim, Chiang Mai 50180, Thailand
phone	+66 53 298-181
web	www.fourseasons.com
capacity	80 rooms
rates	US$425-2,250++

thailand > stay
Four Seasons Resort Chiang Mai

ranking - one-night stand
A full-service resort with everything you would expect from an international chain.

luxe
• Massive residences • Stylish spa
• Cooking school

less luxe
• Pricing • Not exactly close to anywhere special • Looking a bit dated

best for
Lock yourself away for a couple of days pampering and learn how to make your favourite Thai meal.

✱ insider tip
Plan to stay at the cooler time of year, for pleasant evenings and perfect sunny days without stifling humidity.

Triple Two Silom

Whatever Triple Two Silom does, it does it with style. Its long corridors are decorated with original paintings and subtly lit, imparting a cool, quiet air that contrasts completely with the chaotic street outside.

The rooms are surprisingly bright and airy, although the hotel has a limited amount of public space, which means it could start to feel too enclosed after a long stay. A rooftop sitting area would be a nice touch if only it had a plunge-pool for cooling off.

Triple Two has a better street frontage than many hotels on Silom, mainly because it is not under the shadow of the SkyTrain, which diverts away from Silom Road about a block away. While this means the streetfront bar is a nicer place to sit, it does also mean a bit of a hike to the nearest station.

With relatively few rooms, Triple Two Silom feels more inviting than many big city hotels, and the staff actually seem to enjoy themselves on the job, making a stay here a pleasant and welcoming respite.

Triple Two Silom

address	222 Silom Road, Suriyawong, Bangrak, Bangkok 10500, Thailand
phone	+66 2 627-2222
web	www.tripletwosilom.com
capacity	75 rooms
rates	THB5,500-6,900

ranking - one-night stand

Funky address for a Bangkok shopping spree.

luxe

• Smart design • Quiet rooms, despite the busy road outside • Private • Super friendly staff • Small

less luxe

• No pool, but you can use the pool at the ugly tourist hotel next door

best for

Shop till you drop, then sit in the bar and watch the world go by.

✷ insider tip

Upgrade to a suite, particularly if you are planning a long stay.

Tamarind Village

Built around a massive tamarind tree, the 40 rooms at Tamarind Village might not be the most luxurious in Thailand, but they offer a comfortable, peaceful stay in the middle of Chiang Mai.

The polished concrete floors and simple wood furnishings are smart enough, but are let down by basic bathrooms. Nevertheless, the friendly feel of the low-rise development and some pretty lighting in the evenings redeem any flaws. The revamp since our last visit may have made it even better.

Tamarind Village is relatively inexpensive but manages a lot of style: from the bamboo-lined drive to the white orchids in the reception. And it is small enough that even after a short stay, you will feel like part of the family.

Tamarind Village might not be a destination in itself, but for exploring the old part of Chiang Mai, it is easily one of the best choices.

ranking - one-night stand
Rustic but stylish.

luxe
• Brilliant Thai food at ridiculously low prices • Pretty at night

less luxe
• Dowdy bathrooms • Often fully booked

best for
A stylish base from which you can explore Chiang Mai on foot.

✳ insider tip
Book a Superior room, as the only extra with the Deluxe rooms are small balconies.

Tamarind Village
address	50/1 Rajdamnoen Road, Sri Phom, Muang, Chiangmai 50200, Thailand
phone	+66 53 418-896/9
web	www.tamarindvillage.com
capacity	40 rooms
rates	THB4,200-14,000++ (Seasonal)

Stay

Featured Hotels:
- Aleenta Resort and Spa, Hua Hin Pranburi
- Costa Lanta
- Four Seasons Resort Chiang Mai
- The Racha
- Rayavadee
- Sila Evason Hideaway at Samui
- The Sukhothai
- Tamarind Village
- Triple Two Silom
- Twinpalms Phuket

Also:

AMANPURI
+66 76 324-333
Pansea Beach Phuket 83000, Thailand
www.amanresorts.com
The first Aman is in a stunning location and the prices are stunning too — but you get perfectly maintained villas and a fabulous beach.

BANYAN TREE BANGKOK
+66 2 679-1200
21/100 South Sathon Road
Sathon, Bangkok 10120, Thailand
www.banyantree.com
An all-suite hotel sandwiched between the Metropolitan and sensational Sukhothai. The tall tower offers good views, but can feel like an office block.

THE CHEDI PHUKET
+66 76 324-017
118 Moo 3 Choeng Talay, Talang
Phuket 83110, Thailand
www.ghmhotels.com
Pleasant bungalows cascade down to one of the nicest beaches on the island, but the pricing is too high.

THE CONRAD BANGKOK
+66 2 690-9999
87 Wireless Road
Bangkok 10330, Thailand
www.conradhotels.com
One of the newest big international hotels in the heart of Bangkok is creating quite a buzz with its cool bars and eateries and slick rooms.

GRAND HYATT ERAWAN BANGKOK
+66 2 254-1234
494 Rajdamri Road,
Bangkok 10330, Thailand
www.hyatt.com
Right in the heart of the action, the Grand Hyatt is a great choice for a big city hotel. It has stylish new spa-villas on the fifth floor too.

THE ORIENTAL BANGKOK
+66 2 659-9000
48 Oriental Avenue,
Bangkok 10500, Thailand
www.mandarin-oriental.com
Great riverfront setting, but the rooms are not exciting unless you can afford the Authors' Suites in the old part of the hotel.

THE PENINSULA BANGKOK
+66 2 861-2888
333 Charoennakorn Road, Klongsan,
Bangkok 10600, Thailand
www.peninsula.com
Some would say The Peninsula is on the wrong side of the river, but a free shuttle boat takes care of that. River views from all rooms, which are stylish but overly wood-panelled. It's own Philippe Starck-designed eatery.

SALA SAMUI RESORT AND SPA
+66 77 245-888
10/9 Moo 5, Baan Plai Lam Bo Phut, Koh Samui, Suratthani 84320, Thailand
www.salasamui.com
A sexy little resort consisting mainly of walled compounds with villas and plunge pools right on a perfect beach. There are two main beachfront pools and a beach bar too.

Eat

With millions of visitors a year falling in love with Thai food, it is little surprise that Thai restaurants are popping up around the world in the most surprising locations. But few can match the original product.

Given the local water and hygiene standards, you need to take care in choosing where you eat. Unfortunately, it is best to avoid the tempting street food if you want to enjoy the rest of your holiday. But most restaurants offer exquisitely fresh and delicious local cuisine at ridiculously low prices.

Outside of Bangkok, you are less likely to find stylish choices, but you are more likely to find a low-cost local gem.

CELADON
+66 2 344-8888
The Sukhothai Hotel, 13/3 South Sathorn Road, Bangkok, Thailand
It might be part of the Sukhothai Hotel, but Celadon is in a stand-alone building overlooking a lily pond, which makes a truly romantic setting. Service is always excellent, and despite an extensive menu, the food is always exceptional.

EAT ME
+66 2 238-0931
1/6 Piphat Soi 2, Bangkok, Thailand
Really smart restaurant in a side street off Convent Road. It is small, so you will probably need to book ahead. Excellent service, imaginative food and a decent wine-list. A winner.

GREYHOUND CAFÉ
+66 2 664-8663
2nd Floor, Emporium Shopping Complex, Sukhumvit Soi 24, Bangkok, Thailand
Part of a chain, the Greyhound Café in the Emporium is one of the bigger and better offerings and perfect for a break from the shopping. Western-style comfort food is a welcome bonus.

MAHA NAGA
+66 2 662-3060
2 Sukhumvit Soi 29, Bangkok, Thailand
For slick, modern Thai cuisine, served with style, Maha Naga is hard to beat. The stunning conversion of an old villa offers separate dining rooms around a central courtyard. The menu changes and can be hit or miss.

See

A LONG-TAIL BOAT TRIP
You will feel like a tourist, but do hire a long-tail boat for a trip along Bangkok's klongs. It is well worth the effort. You get to see a side of Bangkok life that is visible no other way, as well as enjoying transport not affected by the city's notorious traffic. A fascinating and relatively peaceful diversion.

THE ROYAL PALACE
The royal palace in Bangkok is fascinating. You will have to fight the bussed-in hoards of tourists, so start early and remember to cover up as bare shoulders, midriffs and legs are frowned upon.

CHATUCHAK WEEKEND MARKET
Shopaholics should not miss the Chatuchak weekend market for the opportunity to buy one or more of just about anything. The market is massive, so start with a plan to avoid wandering the endless maze of stalls. Start early.

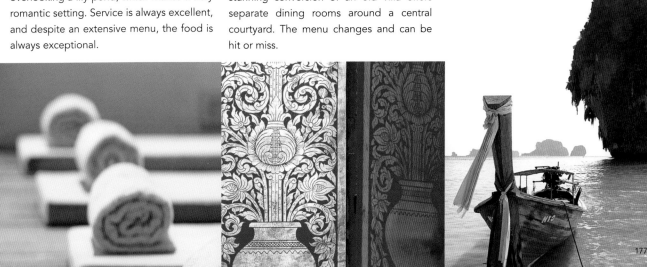

177

>>vietnam

Dissociating Vietnam from the war is not easy, particularly given Hollywood's penchant for rewriting the result over the years. But in Vietnam, the people seem more willing to forgive and forget than the film industry, although the scars are still sometimes painfully obvious.

Still, Vietnam is one of the most charming countries to visit in South-East Asia. Ho Chi Minh City — commonly known as Saigon — is a typically bustling, chaotic big Asian city, but it can still surprise with some great restaurants and quiet museums.

Hanoi though, takes the prize as one of our favourite cities. It is almost completely unspoiled by modern commercialism and revels in its Vietnamese roots and French colonial past. Want a baguette and some really good coffee without the horror of a Starbucks anywhere? Hanoi is the place. Brilliant.

If you are looking for luxury beyond your wildest dreams, you are in the wrong country. Infrastructure is basic, getting around is uncomfortable at best, and there are very few hotels that are destinations in their own right. But for sensationally fresh local food, the occasional decent wine list, great coffee, and stunning scenery Vietnam is hard to beat.

Evason Hideaway at Ana Mandara

In keeping with its environmentally aware policies, Six Senses has only planted native flora but it is a bit sparse, particularly between the villas, which are just too close together for our tastes. However, the villas are fabulous, with so many places to sit that you will probably not get your bottom onto every lounger, daybed or chair in the room.

The resort occupies an entire bay, with its own genuinely private beach. If you must do anything other than laze around, visit a local floating fish farm to select a lobster for dinner. It is worth it — they are the biggest crayfish we have ever seen — although some guests can be a bit squeamish about condemning one to the dinner table.

The service and luxury here would be welcome anywhere, but in Vietnam, where luxurious accommodation barely exists, the Evason Hideaway at Ana Mandara is a godsend.

The Evason people had a little joke when they named this beachside resort. It is a hideaway — the location is miles from anywhere — but it is not really at Ana Mandara.

You will need a break after the effort of getting there, which involves being collected from the internal flight, spending about an hour in a van going to the Ana Mandara Resort at Nha Trang (albeit along a rugged and interesting coastline). From there you spend another half an hour getting to a private jetty followed by yet another half-hour on a speedboat to the Evason Hideaway.

No wonder the place is isolated.

Evason Hideaway at Ana Mandara

address	Beachside Tran Phu Blvd, Nha Trang, Vietnam
phone	+84 58 524-705
web	www.six-senses.com
capacity	55 rooms
rates	US$550-2,000++ (Seasonal)

181

Evason Hideaway at Ana Mandara

ranking - lifetime love
A rare hideaway in bustling Vietnam.

luxe
• Big villas • Isolation

less luxe
• Getting there • Lack of space between villas • High prices

best for
A true escape from the daily grind.

✱ insider tip
Break the journey with a stopover in Ho Chi Minh City or Nha Trang.

183

Victoria Can Tho

The Victoria Can Tho had us fooled at first. The grand building looks as though it has belonged on its spot since colonial times. Not so — it is a relatively new structure, but the ambience is French colonial in all the best ways.

The rooms are functional, if not particularly chic, but the balconies overlooking the river are a fine place to wile away an hour at sunset. The real draw here is the location, right on a bend in the Hau River, a tributary of the Mekong.

The manicured lawn is a perfect place to sit and watch the river traffic pass directly in front of the hotel, which is far enough from the centre of town that there is no passing traffic. Nice.

The Victoria will organise tours of the local area, offering a fascinating glimpse of local life and colour — and that is the main reason to stay there. The hotel is fine, but not a destination in itself.

As a French-operated chain, the food and service are up to international standards, and (thank you, thank you, thank you) it is always a pleasant surprise to get a decent wine list in Asia.

Victoria Can Tho Resort

address	Cai Khe Ward, Ninh Kieu District, Can Tho City, Vietnam
phone	+84 71 810-111
web	www.victoriahotels-asia.com
capacity	92 rooms
rates	US$140-255++ (Seasonal)

Victoria Can Tho Resort

ranking - lost weekend
The only address in this part of Vietnam.

luxe
• Position on the river • European style
• Great service • Quality wine list

less luxe
• Rooms are hardly grand • Getting there
is not fun • Caters to tour groups

best for
This is the only place to stay when exploring
the Mekong Delta.

✱ insider tip
Take the hotel's renovated rice barge
to explore the floating markets. You will
have to get out of bed early, but it is
worth the effort.

187

Sofitel Metropole Hanoi

ranking - one-night stand
The smartest address in Hanoi.

luxe
• Central location • Sense of history
• Service

less luxe
• New Opera Wing lacks charm

best for
Exploring exotic Hanoi.

✳ insider tip
Take to the city on foot and take your credit card — there is unique shopping here.

Sofitel Metropole Hanoi
address   15 Ngo Quyen Street
          10000 Hanoi, Vietnam
phone   +84 4 826-6919
web   www.accorhotels-asia.com
capacity 235 rooms
rates   US$119-1,584++

The Metropole is another of South-East Asia's grande dame hotels, which can be a boon or a bane, depending on your point of view.

It is better maintained than most hotels in Vietnam (although it was said to have become a little tatty recently) and the management tends to be very professional. However, the rooms in the new wing can barely match the old ones for sheer charm and the pool area is likely to be crowded.

Stay in the Historical Wing rather than the New Opera Wing, but be aware that not all suites in the Historical Wing are equal either and even suites with separate sitting areas do not guarantee plenty of space.

The flip side is that the hotel is nice. It is in a brilliant location, within walking distance of Hanoi's most interesting tourist sites and shopping. And you can arrange a shopping tour in the hotel's restored vintage Citroën.

If you plan to explore Hanoi's charming historical quarter, there is no better base than this.

189

Stay

Featured Hotels:
- Evason Hideaway at Ana Mandara
- Sofitel Metropole Hanoi
- Victoria Can Tho Resort

Also:

CARAVELLE HOTEL
+84 8 823-4999
19 Lam Son Square, District 1,
Ho Chi Minh City, Vietnam
www.caravellehotel.com
Right in the middle of the historic district, the Caravelle is a legend, although it is difficult to tell why from its external appearance. One of the best club floors anywhere.

HILTON HANOI OPERA
+84 4 933-0500
1 Le Thanh Tong Street,
Hanoi, Vietnam
www.hilton.com
The Hilton Hanoi Opera is in a great location and the exterior was designed to be sympathetic with the surrounds, although the rooms are not that special. Go for the executive floor.

PARK HYATT SAIGON
+84 8 824-1234
2 Lam Son Square, District 1,
Ho Chi Minh City, Vietnam
www.hyatt.com
The newly opened Park Hyatt is impressing people and rightly so: it has a great location, it is stylish and well run too.

Eat

Food in Vietnam is a delight. The Vietnamese have a distinctive local cuisine that values fresh ingredients. And there are great culinary relics from French colonial times such as decent coffee, bread and wine lists.

AU LAC CAFÉ
+84 4 825-7807
57 Ly Thai To Street, Hoan Kiem District, Hanoi, Vietnam
A pleasant little café in a courtyard setting that is perfect for a casual lunch. Excellent Vietnamese food or baguettes and coffee — you decide.

EMPEROR
+84 4 826-8801
18b Le Than Tong Street, Hoan Kiem District, Hanoi, Vietnam

A restored villa restaurant with plenty of tables, which is popular because of its good service and great food (particularly if you have Vietnamese friends with you who can order the best dishes).

WILD RICE
+84 4 943-8896
6 Ngo Thi Nham Street, Hoan Kiem District, Hanoi, Vietnam
The décor is modern Vietnam at its best: a restored villa with a funky glassed-in room at the rear. Excellent service and wine list, but food can vary in quality.

QUAN AN NGON
+84 8 825-7179
138 Nam Khoi Nghia, District 1, Ho Chi Minh City, Vietnam
Incredibly popular with the local lunchtime crowd — and for good reason. It is housed in an old villa with cooking stations around the outside wall and the food is cheap, cheerful and very, very good.

TEMPLE CLUB
+84 8 829-9244
29 Thon That Thiep, District 1, Ho Chi Minh City, Vietnam
Walk up a flight of stairs from an ordinary street into this exceptional restaurant.

Excellent Vietnamese fare, great service and a good wine list.

See

Don't make the mistake of thinking you will see all of Vietnam in one trip — there is so much of it.

HALONG BAY

It is well worth the effort to make the long daytrip from Hanoi to Halong Bay. The UNESCO World Heritage-listed bay is dotted with thousands of limestone islands and is an amazing sight. It can be explored in comfort too — avoid the crowds and hire a boat for yourself. You will get a crew, including a cook who will whip up some fresh seafood and you have the freedom to stop wherever you want. Plus the road journey there through picturesque countryside is fascinating.

HANOI

Hanoi's heritage areas are great places to explore on foot, although the best time for this is in the cool season — the humidity is oppressive in the hot season. Much of the city is run down, but there are boutiques and homeware shops that are imaginative and original. And there are no McDonald's or Starbucks anywhere — surely the only major city in the region where this is the case.

THE MEKONG DELTA

From Ho Chi Minh City, the Mekong Delta is accessible (see Victoria Can Tho) but the trip is not glamorous. Exploring the river and tributaries by boat is the way to go. The floating markets are genuine, not sideshows staged for tourists.